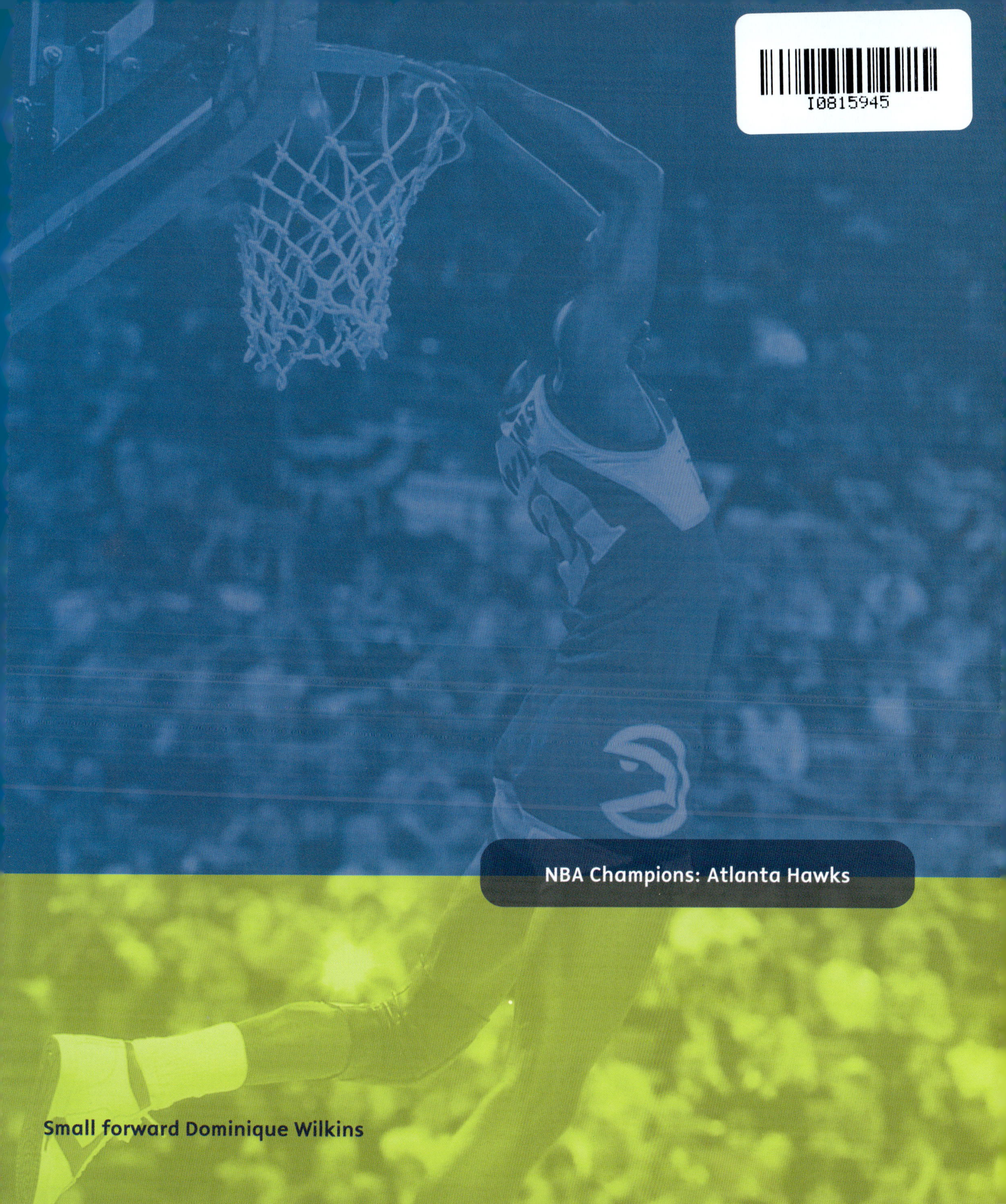

Small forward Dominique Wilkins

Center Tree Rollins

NBA CHAMPIONS

ATLANTA HAWKS

BY JOE TISCHLER

CREATIVE EDUCATION / CREATIVE PAPERBACKS

Power forward Alexander Volkov

Published by Creative Education and Creative Paperbacks
P.O. Box 227, Mankato, Minnesota 56002
Creative Education and Creative Paperbacks are imprints of The Creative Company
www.thecreativecompany.us

Art Direction by Tom Morgan
Book production by Graham Morgan
Edited by Grace Cain

Images by Associated Press/AP Photo, 7, 12; Getty Images/Andrew D. Bernstein, cover, 1, Fernando Medina, 6, Focus On Sport, 2, George Long/WireImage, 15, Icon Sports Wire, 3, Jason Miller, 24, John Biever, 16, Kevin C. Cox, 5, New York Daily News Archive, 19, Sporting News Archive, 4, Thearon W. Henderson, cover, Todd Kirkland, 10, 20; Unsplash/Brad Huchteman, 9

Library of Congress Cataloging-in-Publication Data
Names: Tischler, Joe, author.
Title: Atlanta Hawks / by Joe Tischler.
Description: Mankato, Minnesota : Creative Education and Creative Paperbacks, [2025] | Series: Creative sports: NBA champions | Includes index. | Audience: Ages 7-10 | Audience: Grades 2-3 | Summary: "Elementary-level text and dynamic sports photos highlight the NBA championship win of the Atlanta Hawks, plus sensational players associated with the professional basketball team such as Trae Young"—Provided by publisher.
Identifiers: LCCN 2024014018 (print) | LCCN 2024014019 (ebook) | ISBN 9798889892496 (library binding) | ISBN 9781682776155 (paperback) | ISBN 9798889893608 (ebook)
Subjects: LCSH: Atlanta Hawks (Basketball team)—History—Juvenile literature. | Basketball players—United States—Juvenile literature.
Classification: LCC GV885.52.A7 T57 2025 (print) | LCC GV885.52.A7 (ebook) | DDC 796.323/6409758231—dc23/eng/20240404
LC record available at https://lccn.loc.gov/2024014018
LC ebook record available at https://lccn.loc.gov/2024014019

Printed in China

Power forward Paul Millsap

Center Al Horford

CONTENTS

Home of the Hawks

Atlanta is the largest city in the state of Georgia. It's also the state capital. The world's busiest airport is there. Also there is State Farm **Arena**. It's where the Hawks basketball team plays their home games.

The Atlanta Hawks are a National Basketball Association (NBA) team. They compete in the Southeast Division. That's part of the Eastern Conference. Their **rivals** are the Miami Heat and Orlando Magic. All NBA teams want to win the NBA Finals and become champions.

EMORY

Point guard Trae Young

Naming the Hawks

he team once played their home games in the Midwest. They were called the Tri-Cities Blackhawks. They represented cities in both Illinois and Iowa. In the 1830s, there was a Sauk Indian Chief named Black Hawk. He once led a war in the region. The team name was shortened to Hawks when the club moved to Milwaukee, Wisconsin, in 1951.

Center Bob Pettit

Hawks History

The Hawks entered the NBA in 1949. They weren't very good in either the Tri-Cities or Milwaukee. They finally started playing well in another home, St. Louis, Missouri. They moved there in 1955. Center Bob Pettit was one of the team's first stars. He was an **all-star** all 11 years he played for the Hawks. Twice he was named NBA **Most Valuable Player (MVP)**.

Pettit led the Hawks to the NBA Finals in 1957. They lost to the Boston Celtics. The following year, the two teams met again in the Finals. This time, the Hawks won! The Hawks returned to the Finals in 1960 and 1961. Both times they lost to the Celtics.

In 1968, the Hawks moved again. They went to Atlanta. Lou Hudson was the team's first star in Atlanta. He helped the team to the Western Division Finals two years in a row.

Shooting guard Lou Hudson

Small forward Dominique Wilkins

Dominique Wilkins was the team's next great star. He was known for his high-flying **slam dunks**. Wilkins's nickname was the "Human Highlight Film." He won two NBA Slam Dunk Contests. He also played in nine All-Star Games.

Lenny Wilkens was a great player and coach for the Hawks. He was an all-star point guard for nine seasons. Later he was the team's head coach for seven seasons. Despite all of this talent, the Hawks haven't been back to the NBA Finals in over 60 years.

Other Hawks Stars

The Hawks have had many other stars. Mookie Blaylock and Wayne "Tree" Rollins were great defenders. Blaylock stole passes. Rollins blocked shots. Dikembe Mutombo was great on defense as well. Twice he was named NBA Defensive Player of the Year for the Hawks.

Center Dikembe Mutombo

Shooting guard Dejounte Murray

Power forward Cliff Hagan played great in the St. Louis years. He played in five All-Star Games. Guard Joe Johnson scored a lot of points in the 2000s. He was an all-star six times.

Trae Young is one of the game's best scorers today. He makes a lot of three-point shots. Dejounte Murray scores a lot, too. Hawks fans hope they can help bring a **title** to Atlanta soon!

About the Hawks

First season: 1946–47

Conference/division: Eastern Conference, Southeast Division

Team colors: red, yellow, black, and gray

Home arena: State Farm Arena

NBA CHAMPIONSHIPS:

1958, 4 games to 2 over Boston Celtics

TEAM WEBSITE:

https://www.nba.com/hawks/

Glossary

all-star—a player picked to play in the All-Star Game, featuring the season's top stars

arena—a large building with seats for spectators, where sports games and entertainment events are held

Most Valuable Player (MVP)—an honor given to the season's best player

rival—a team that plays extra hard against another team

slam dunk—a shot that is thrown hard through the hoop

title—another word for championship

Point guard Jeff Teague

Index